TINY HOUSE TALES

IN THEIR OWN WORDS

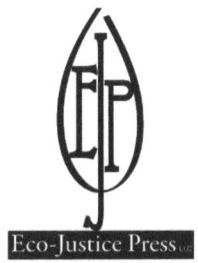

Copyright © 2025 Alexander Daniell

shelternoweugene.org

All rights reserved. No part of this book may be reproduced or transmitted in any form or by any means electronic or mechanical including photocopying, recording, or by any information storage and retrieval system without permission in writing from the publisher or author.

Eco-Justice Press, L.L.C.
P.O. Box 5409 Eugene, OR 97405
www.ecojusticepress.com

Tiny House Tales
By Alexander Daniell

Library of Congress Control Number: 2025932123
ISBN 978-1-945432-68-2

EDITED BY
ALEXANDER DANIELL

As Rilke said:

*"You must give birth to your images.
They are the future waiting to be born.
Fear not the strangeness you feel.
The future must enter you long before it happens."*

Budget Bungalow

I am the Budget Bungalow. I was born from the leftover scraps of a great student dorm. One square block of leafy neighborhood was bulldozed to make room for its seven floors. The framing from its foundation forms, the plywood cut-outs from its windows, these are my bones. I am the Budget Bungalow.

I am the first, the prototype of prototypes, the first Tiny House that my mother birthed for the first Tiny House village for the homeless.

My pieces were built in my mother's Yurt, and assembled by homeless volunteers in the parking lot of a church. I stand still, ten years later, number nine at Opportunity Village Eugene.

I am windows and a door. I am beams that carry the weight of the ceiling and the floor. I am air and light, transforming sunlight into warmth through my skylight.

I am a soft warm bed, a chair and a lamp and a desk and a drawer, a safe space from the rain and the cold of a long winter's night behind a locked door. I am shelter.

I am small enough to be moved from one place to another, when I have overstayed my welcome. I am large enough to turn and stretch with arms swinging outward, large enough for elbows and knees, large enough for company. I can transform the dark sodden figure of a ghost laboring down the roadside beneath a bag of bottles into a man.

I belong to no one. I belong to everyone. I have been blessed by a minister. I am an example of what is possible. I am one less homeless man on the street. I am the Budget Bungalow.

3

CLUBHOUSE

I am the Clubhouse. Second born, I too have my brothers and sisters at Opportunity Village. I too am built of pieces and my womb was the Yurt. But I give shelter to shovels and spades, rakes and hoes and wheelbarrows. I live at the University of Oregon Urban Garden.

The Urban Garden will die and so will I.

There are two university Urban Gardens in our city, the creation of an inspired teacher and many university students who crave the opportunity to take their eyes off the computer screen and plunge their hands into the dirt.

The Urban Garden by the river, with its majestic hand-hewn barn, already lies in the shadow of the new glass and steel Institute for the Accelerated Application of Scientific Research. Trees beside the barn have been cut for ease of building another tower. My Urban Garden is beside the playground behind the ice cream shop. But the University has bought all the houses for three blocks down. So it is only a matter of time.

Ours is a city of Urban Gardens. The houses' lots, with their sprawling yards of fruit trees and vegetables, will be cut in half and cut in half again. But for now they are dotted with hundreds of tiny houses, like me, that shelter children who can not afford the new rents, the old and the infirm without any family, the brothers and sisters gone awry. There are many more like me. I am in good company. I am the Clubhouse.

Pagoda

I was a mistake. The third and last Tiny House birthed in the Yurt. As the saw was whining and the drill was whirring, melding the pieces of my frame, my mother heard a voice calling:

"Alex! Alex! Come here!"

My mother stepped outside, still holding his drill. His next door neighbor, Amon, was standing there. Amon was a striking hawk nosed Israeli gentleman in his mid-eighties with a gold earring, who lived next door to my mother. He gently grasped my mother's arm and pulled him aside. He glanced around carefully, to see that no one else was listening.

"Alex", he said "The neighbors, they are talking. 'Why?', they say,' so much noise?' They are hippies, I say. They stay up late and zey get up late. They work from noon to eight. But the neighbors Alex. The neighbors are still talking."

So my mother had to go rent a shop. But at first there was no place for me, so I was put together on the front lawn of a hippie commune where my mother used to live, just down the street from my brother, the Clubhouse, in the Urban Garden. A young man who lived in the commune dreamed up Opportunity Village, where my brothers and sisters and I would eventually live. He put a sign out telling of the village. He shot a time-lapse video of the pieces of my soul being put together. He was a hippie.

But I was a mistake. Though I looked cute in the pictures of the volunteers putting me up in the village, I was too small and dark inside. Plus I had no room for a loft. So I had only one twin in the village.

Lean To

I am the Lean To, and I was not a mistake. The fourth and final prototype approved by the city of Eugene for Opportunity Village, I was an afterthought of my mother's.

My mother could design and build, but he didn't know how to draw. He had a friend, a generous architect, who would take his rough sketches and finished models and turn them into ground plans and elevations and exploded axion views. These my mother would enlarge, hand-notate, and post on the walls of his shop for volunteers to study. These he would also submit to the city. I know all this because I heard him talking.

It was late in the game, the eleventh hour, when my mother brought his chicken scratchings of me into the architect's office. There were many things to do to turn the dream of my mother's into reality.

My mother had a meeting the next day with the Lutherans of Thrivent Financial Corporation, who had agreed to donate six thousand dollars for the materials to build me and my three siblings at Opportunity Village. They also agreed to provide several dozen Lutheran volunteers wearing green Thrivent t-shirts to put us together. When my mother arrived at the meeting in the basement of the Episcopal Church of the Resurrection the plans he handed out were still warm.

The architect did a beautiful drawing of me, fixing all my mother's oversights, but I still almost died that morning, along with my sisters and brothers. The Lutherans are a practical bunch, and some of them thought that all the tiny houses at Opportunity Village should be the same, in neat tidy rows, for efficiency. But Janet Howe, who had the original idea to hit up her boss in the office for the six thousand, stood up and said that if my mother thought that we should have four different designs, that if he thought we should arrange the Tiny Houses around courtyards rather than in straight lines, then that is what we should do. Because of Janet Howe I, and my brothers and sisters, got to live.

I am the Lean To. My loft is tall and broad, high enough to sit up in and long enough to sleep in. My roof-line is offset, providing a covered porch. As the village grew, people chose the houses they liked best, and my mother built more of them. I was the most popular. And so though I had several twins I also had cousins that were bigger, and had dormers, with extra windows and wider overhangs than I had. But I was the first, from my mother's last minute chicken scratchings, and I am proud of that. I am the Lean To.

Lean To

Alexander Daniell, Designer\Owner ~ Eugene, Oregon

REGISTERED ARCHITECT
WILLARD C. DIXON
EUGENE, OREGON
STATE OF OREGON

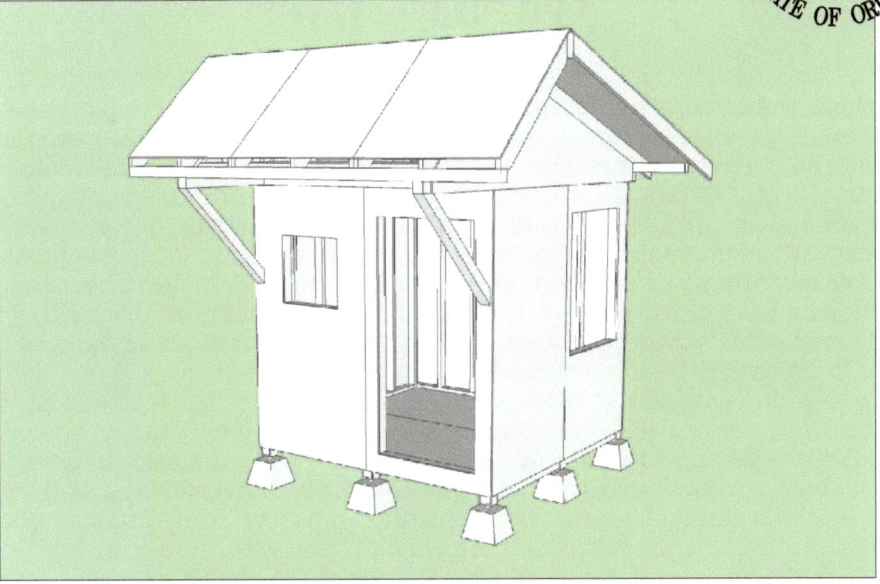

Kit of Parts Study, PERSPECTIVE VIEW

(A) scale: For Reference Only

LEAN TO

WILLARD C. DIXON Architect, AIA

300 BLAIR BLVD.
EUGENE, OR. 97402-4150
PHONE: 541.689.3548
FAX: 1.541.982.2273 (all #s)
CELL: 541.868.5960

DES: AD
DRF: YL / TMS
DATE: 06-03-13
REV:

LEAN TO
Alexander Daniell, Owner ~ Eugene, Oregon
Kit of Parts Study, PERSPECTIVE VIEW

© 2013 WILLARD C. DIXON Architect, LLC

1/2

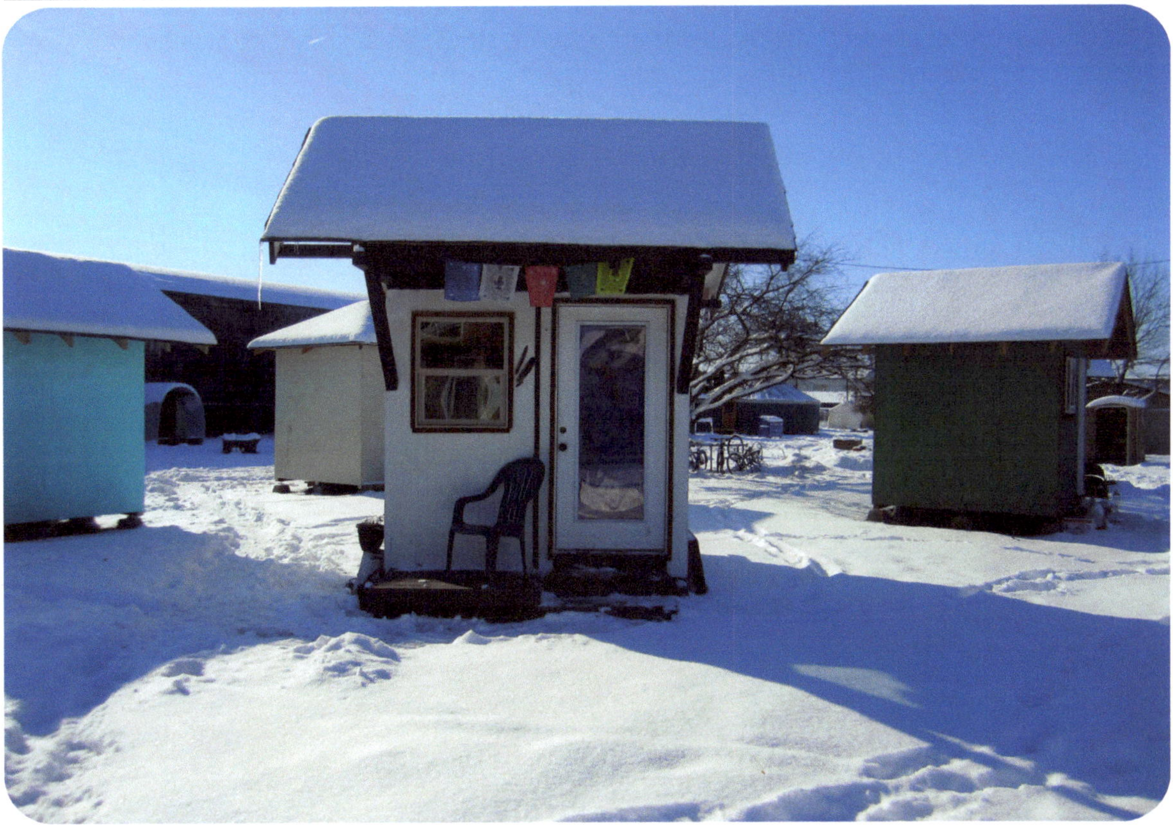

Cyclops

I am the Cyclops, the great granddaughter of the first Lean To. My three great aunts, the Clubhouse, the Budget Bungalow, and the Pagoda; as well as my great-grandfather, the Lean To, were all built on the first day. We were built by the Graduate Student from the commune, and the Big Kahuna, and the Lutherans; under the direction of my mother.

Before we were built people were afraid of us, and what we would become, a dreary gray camp sheltering the homeless. But when they saw our peaks and turrets painted in bright colors their fears diminished. They were not expecting a Caribbean beach village.

I am the Cyclops. I have one great eye, a donated Palladian window, protruding from my extended dormer, with a sweeping view of the great courtyard. And I must tell you, in my ten years here, there are some strange things that I have seen.

Once there was a man screaming at the gate: "Someone stole my bicycle! I know it's here!" So the gate was opened and the man, wearing a baseball cap, marched through the courtyard. He looked and looked, but all he saw were the villagers, trimming the grass, sweeping their porches, and weeding the big planters overflowing with strawberries. The blue and green and orange houses smiled down on him, and the villagers smiled at him too. "I'm sorry," he said, marching back to the gate. "I'm so sorry."

Another time my mother and his friend who is an artist snuck in under cover of darkness. They had a powerful slide projector and set it up to shine images on our walls. The images were the black outlines of animal totems, Eagles and Salmon and Otters and Bears. One of the artists held the projector while the other traced thick lines in black ink. Later the villagers colored them in with the colors they liked.

I am the Cyclops, and there is no other house like me. But in truth, no two houses are the same at Opportunity Village.

Opportunity Village Eugene
Pioneering New Solutions for the (Formerly) Homeless

By Alex Daniell

Opportunity Village Eugene is Eugene, Oregon's newest intentional community. In less than three months, in late summer and fall of 2013, for less than $60,000, it went from an empty public works parking lot to a village housing 30 people. There have been many players, major and minor, male and female, straight and gay; organizers, volunteers, and villagers themselves. It is a self-governing village, with oversight and veto power over Village Council decisions by the board of the nonprofit organization Opportunity Village Eugene, which is chaired by Dan Bryant, minister of the First Congregational Church downtown.

Opportunity Village (www.opportunityvillageeugene.org) is governed by the Village Manual and its Village Agreements (www.opportunityvillageeugene.org/p/community-agreement.html). The Village Manual is an improved version of similar documents written by the residents of other homeless camps, like Dignity Village and Right to Dream Two in Portland, Oregon. It is authored by Andy Heben, who is also the urban designer of Opportunity Village.

Nine Conestoga Huts, insulated vinyl-sheathed shelters made from a combination of reused and new materials, were built in the village by Community Supported Shelters (communitysupportedshelters.org). I have designed, and built with the help of many others, all 18 of the solid-walled buildings in the village, including dwellings, a bath house, a kitchen, a front office, and also an outdoor grill. Like the Village Manual, the Backyard Bungalows (hebenaj.wix.com/backyardbungalows) we've built are improved versions of the dwellings erected by residents of other homeless villages. They are modular designs, composed of panels that are constructed in the shop and assembled on site in big work parties.

In July I submitted four of these prototypes, all under 100 square feet, with interchangeable wall and roof systems, to the city of Eugene and the state of Oregon for pre-approval to house the homeless. All four were accepted without any alterations. I now have nearly a dozen prototypes that have passed inspection by the city.

Ted Drummond, a longtime leader in the First Christian Church's annual house-building Mission to Mexico, erected a heated 30-foot yurt for the villagers just days before the early-December snows came. Andy, Ted, and I are partners in the micro-housing business I founded in 2012, called Backyard Bungalows. Our mission is to build Affordable Villages, after the model of Opportunity Village.

When the city of Eugene broke up the Occupy camp in December of 2011, they promised to give the homeless another piece of land. Dan Bryant, a minister who wears a leather jacket and drives a motorcycle, Jean Stacey, a fiery

Bath House

I am the Bath House at Opportunity Village. My skeleton murmurs with electricity. My veins pulse with hot and cold running water. A washing machine whirrs. Toilets flush. I am clean skin, fresh clothes, bright white shining teeth. I am what separates man from beast.

At first they didn't want me. But my mother, and the Graduate Student from the commune, and the architects, and the Big Kahuna, they all kept at the city. I think they didn't want me because I was illegal. I think they didn't want me because they didn't want the people at Opportunity Village to stay, and if there was no Bath House, they might not stay. But when the Rotary Club gave the money to build me, they couldn't say no.

I have two flush toilets, a shower and a washer and a dryer inside 114 square feet, which is just six feet less than the maximum size of an auxiliary storage unit permitted on a commercial lot. For you see - all my brothers and sisters and aunts and uncles are not dwelling units but auxiliary storage units. That is how we are allowed to exist. Because we, like the people from the street who are stored inside us, do not count. We do not count because we are not counted. Therefore, technically, we do not exist. And if we do not exist we can not be illegal. For something can not be illegal if it does not exist.

I am built to last. My floor is a single sheet of thick vinyl. My walls are half inch plywood, painted with several layers of eggshell white. My shower is used two dozen times a day. After seven years and fifty thousand showers, my mother unscrewed the outside wall and John the Plumber put in a new shower.

I am proud of myself. I have given cleanliness, and a sense of solace, to thirty people a day. I am the Bath House.

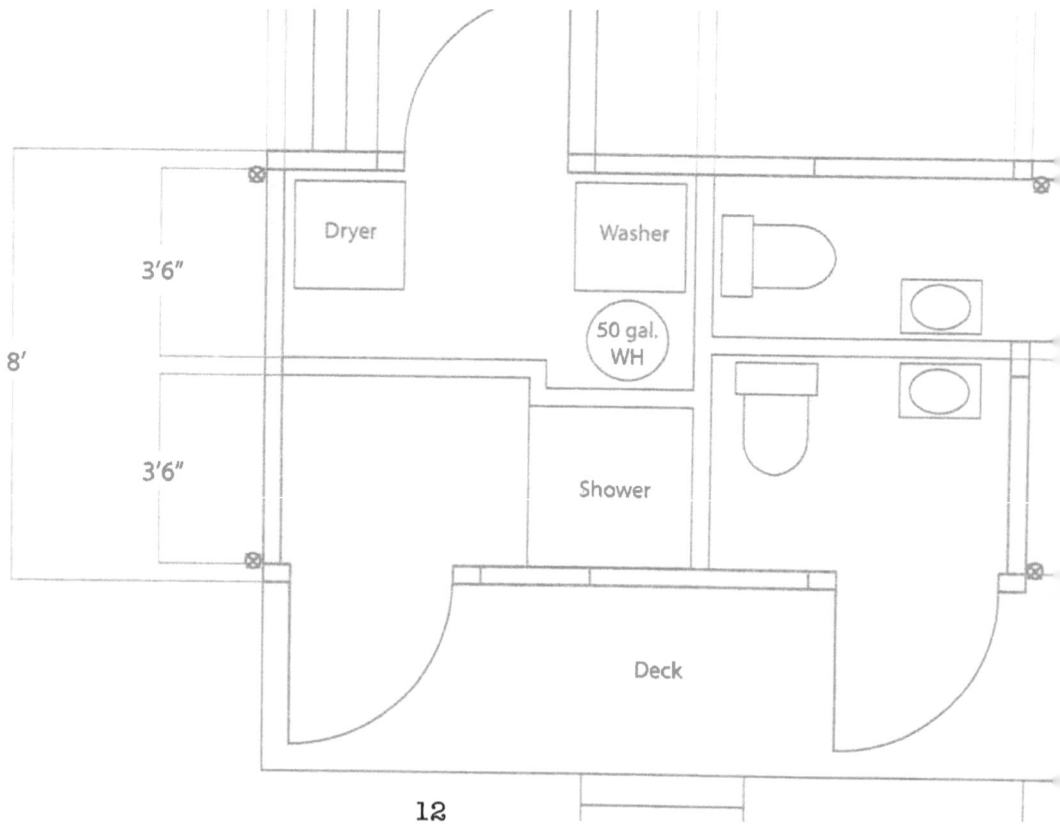

Gate House

I am the Gate House at Opportunity Village. I am tall, and I am strong, and I hear all. Someone is inside me twenty-four hours a day, 365 days a year. The villagers staff me themselves. Everyone takes a shift. They do not want aggressive people in the village.

There was once an aggressive man who lived in the village. He liked to sit on my stoop, smoking cigarettes. He liked to patrol the perimeter of the village in his camo gear, looking for intruders and checking for holes in the fence. He liked to tell people what to do, once he got his turn on the village council. He liked to boss people around, especially other men. He liked to protect women. And because he was so aggressive, he got voted out of the village.

The next day the Big Kahuna got a call from the city. Someone had left an anonymous message complaining that live extension cords were draped through the puddles at the village, and that the villagers were not safe. So the Big Kahuna, and my mother, and the Graduate Student from the commune down the street, were all summoned before the Fire Marshall, and the Police Chief, and the top building inspector of the city.

In many another city, this would have been enough to shut down the village. In most other cities Opportunity Village would never have been allowed to be built. But by the warmth and graciousness of our people, by the tolerance of our officials, by the slight of hand of our city attorney, Opportunity Village was allowed to live, and all my brothers and sisters became examples to other cities.

As my mother and his brothers sat before their judges, they spoke of health and safety. They spoke of meeting the intent of the building code in all ways possible under a small budget. They promised that the extension cords would be removed. And they took the officials on a tour of the village.

By the time the tour was over, the Fire Marshall and my mother were sketching a design for the outdoor kitchen.

I am the Gate House. I am the guardian of the village. The village has a right to exist, even if it does not exist on paper. The people of the village have a right to exist, even if they do not exist on the census. I am the Gate House, and I will guard the village.

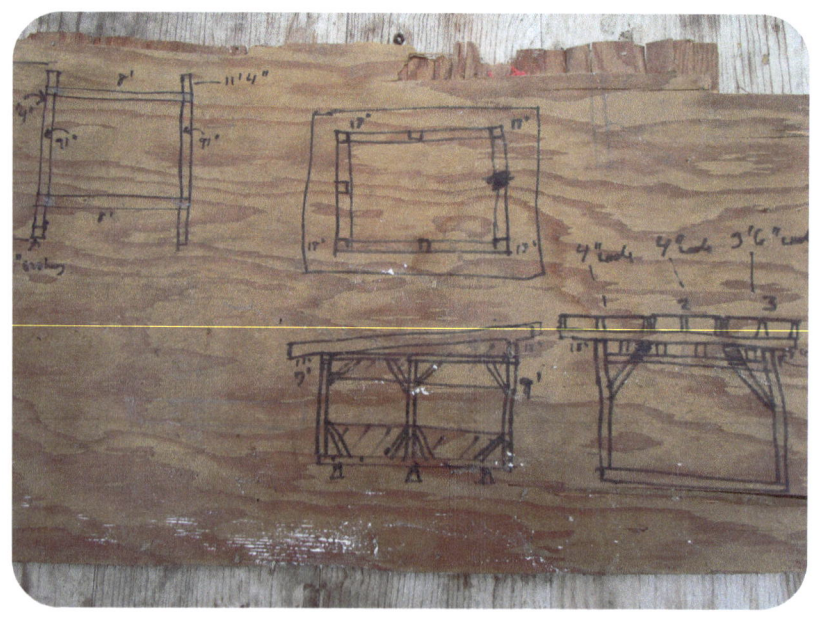

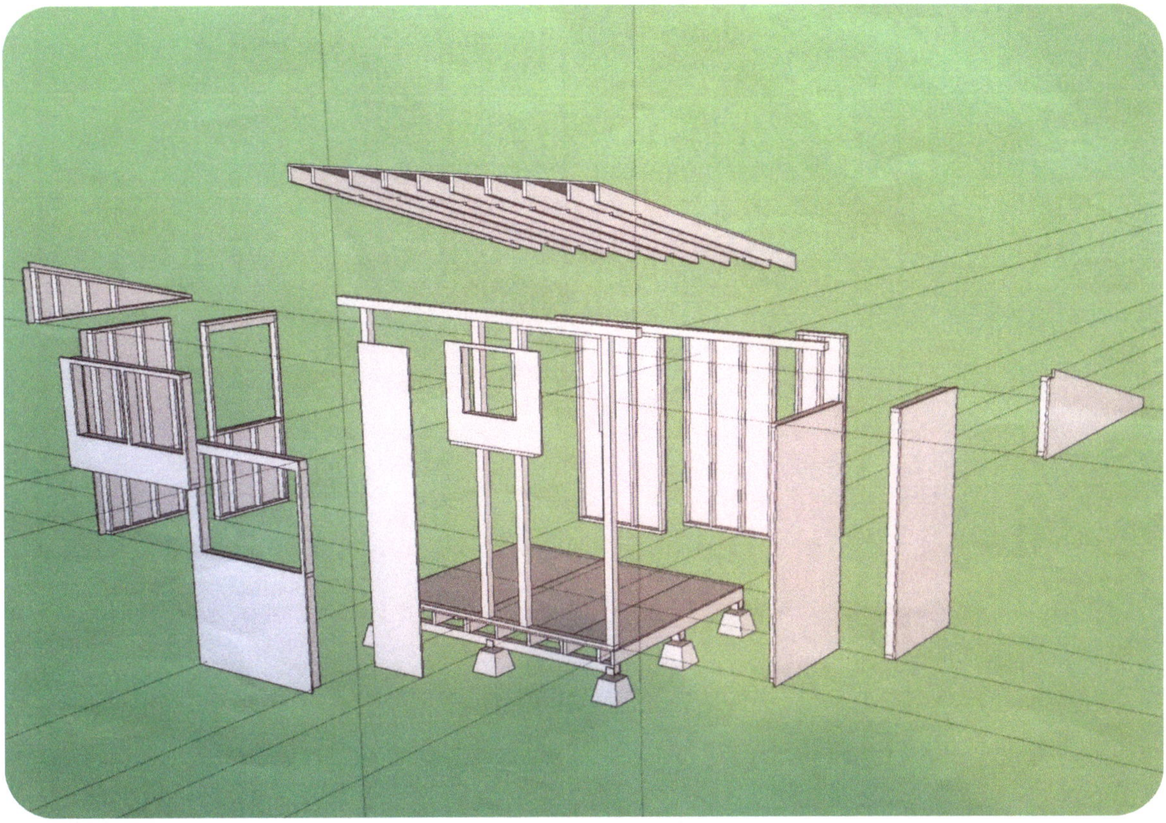

Outdoor Kitchen

I am the Outdoor Kitchen, born when my mother drew a sketch with the Fire Marshall. I am a gas grill with a roof and a floor. I have storage shelves, counter tops, and four open walls. The Fire Marshall asked my mother if there would be unsupervised villagers cooking bacon and igniting grease fires late at night. My mother said probably. That is why I have open walls. So that if the flames rise up the villagers can back away and escape. I am not very tall.

What the Fire Marshall told my mother he most fears is the "lawn bomb." With the rare exception of a house filling with natural gas and blowing up, the lawn bomb is the most common form of residential mayhem. A lawn bomb is a propane tank with a rubber hose that gets cut by a weed whacker and sparks an explosion. That is why my gas tank is twelve feet from me in its own little doghouse. It has a regulator on the top to stop down the pressure, and a solid steel gas line that runs underground and has a shut off valve underneath my grill.

I love the people who gather within me to cook and eat. I love my brother to my left and my sister to my right. Both are Clubhouses. My sister is plumbed and wired and has a sink. She sets next to my uncle, the Bath House. My brother is the pantry.

My brother and my sister, like all my mother's children at Opportunity Village, are built on movable pier pads, a foot off the ground. Our floors are framed with pressure-treated lumber, which does not rot. There is no skirting, so the air can circulate underneath. Nothing is allowed to be stored beneath us. This is so that were a mouse or a rat to try to nest up underneath they would have no cover, and would most certainly be caught by a cat. At Opportunity Village there are no mice or rats.

All our counter tops are sanitized and wiped clean. Temperatures in the refrigerators and freezer are monitored daily. Dry goods are stored in sealed plastic tubs on pallets off the floor which are inventoried daily, last in first out, so that nothing has the chance to spoil. My brother and sister and I run a tight ship. We are the Outdoor Kitchen.

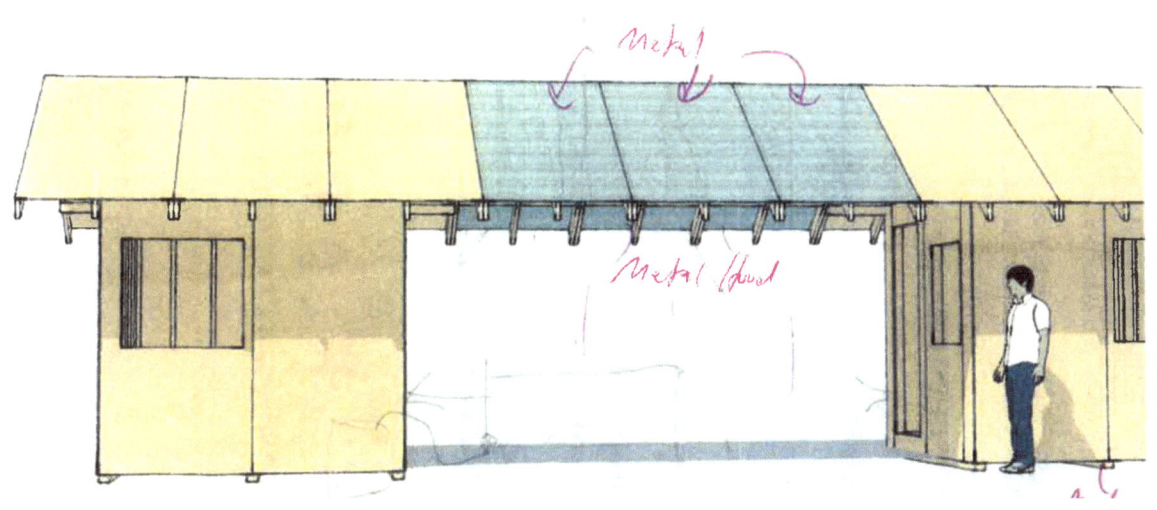

FIREHOUSE

I am the Firehouse. I was built with money donated by three different fire departments. I am red and black. My mother built me with an overhanging loft, because the old firehouses had lofts to store hay for their horses.

One gray day in May, all three fire departments came to paint me. They painted not just me, but the unfinished parts of many of my brothers and sisters, uncles and aunts. They were beautiful strong men, and they cut in perfectly with their brushes. They lifted great rocks to line the paths, and dragged heavy planters to where the villagers wanted them. They offered to come to my mother's shop between shifts, and build more members of the family for the village. At one point all three captains stood together and talked with my mother. Their chins jutted out and they were very handsome. The shortest one towered, at six feet three inches, above my mother.

The firemen were happy to come and work, but they were disappointed that the villagers did not come out to help, as they had said they would. The villagers became sheepish and scared and snuck out before the firemen arrived, to smoke cigarettes in the nooks and crannies of the streets. For you see, the firemen were strong and the villagers were weak. The firemen were confident and the villagers were meek. The firemen were successful and the villagers were failures. The firemen represented to the villagers all the things that they could never be. And because the villagers did not come out to help, as the firemen had thought they would, the firemen felt betrayed and did not come back to help at the village.

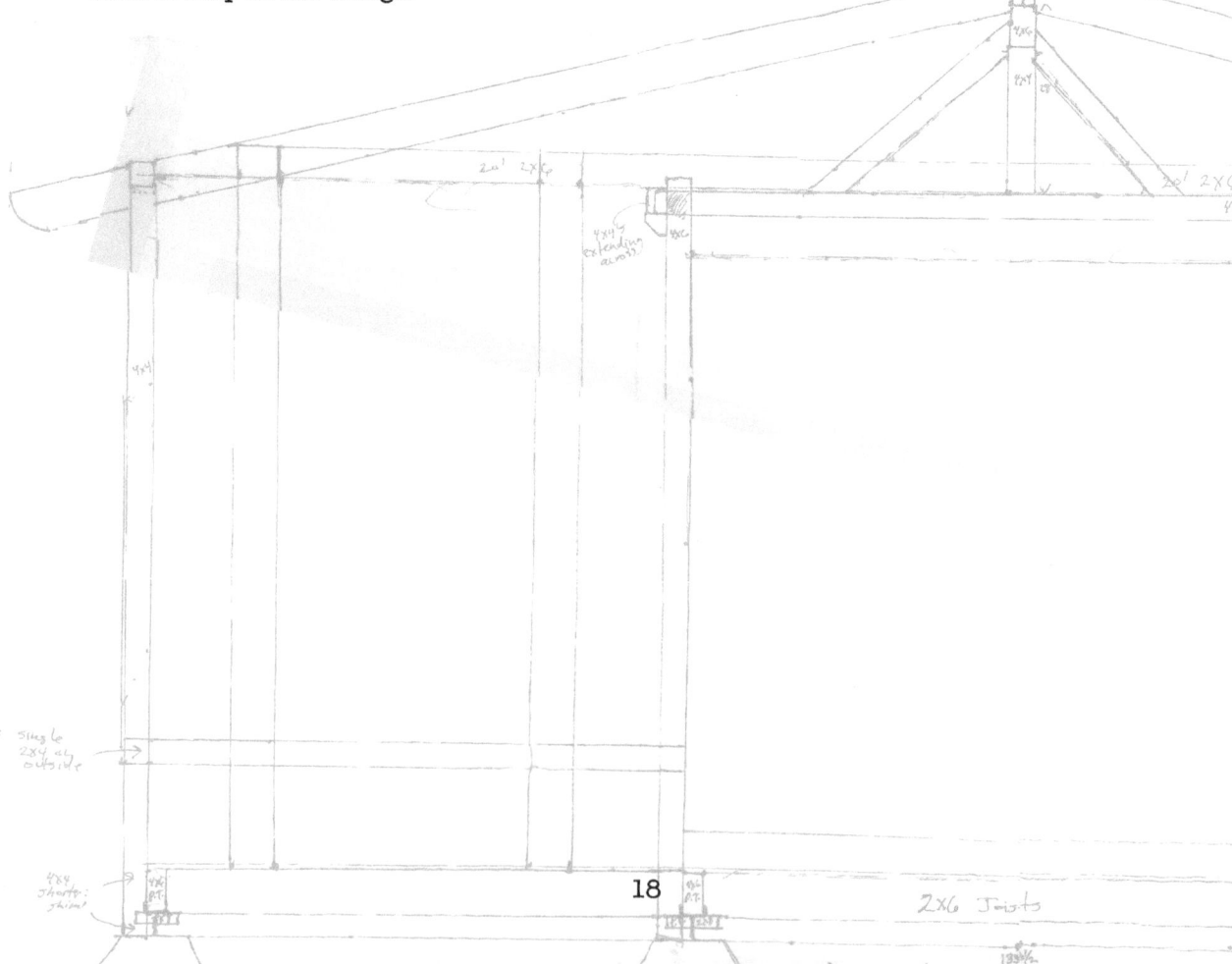

...and a place to call home.

First Family Cabin

I am the First Family Cabin, the first tiny house that my mother built on wheels. His idea was to make me movable, so that I could provide shelter for someone in a church parking lot, under the St. Vincent de Paul Car-Camper Program. The Central Lutheran Church agreed to adopt me. My mother built me with a big shiny trailer hitch sticking out of my rear end, so that everyone knew that if they became tired of me that I could easily be moved away.

As I said I was built on wheels, but the wheels were not very good. My mother didn't have much money, so he went to a junk yard and found a rusty single axle trailer with two good wheels for two hundred dollars. But a tiny house needs four wheels, not two. Plus my mother built me with a tall peaked roof. So I was tippy from the start.

There were three volunteers who helped my mother build me. One was a tree planter and one was an astronomer and one was a homeless man. One morning there was an accident. The homeless man knocked a drill off my roof and it fell on the astronomer's head. The astronomer was all right, but my mother had to fire the homeless man, which wasn't very nice. The astronomer never came back, but the tree planter stayed and a truck driver came to help, so I got finished.

I am the First Family Cabin. I am tall and I am strong, with a big window in my back and a cozy porch off my front. There is enough room inside me for a loft. At first I was the apple of my mother's eye. But over time my paint faded, and my mother had other children. But I know that he admires me still when he drives by.

The House of Sin

I am the House of Sin. I have gone through many phases of my life, like many of my kin. I was begun with the best of intentions, but descended into darkness and was unwanted. For a time I belonged to no one but God.

My mother birthed me as a project of the local Community College. I was a vehicle for students to learn all the tricks of the trade in a small and inexpensive way. Then I was to be gifted to a local church to house one of their parishioners, a homeless man named Cowboy.

My mother and the shop teacher put up the money for materials to build me, along with some funds from the Community College. The students building me had a grand time, and they all got on the front page of the college newspaper.

But things at the church went awry. The priest who worked with my mother got into some trouble and had to leave. The homeless man named Cowboy fled back to Texas and left my door open. The junkies moved in, burning candles and joints, shooting heroin, cooking and smoking meth. By the time the church noticed, my inside was unspeakable. They bolted the door and threw away the key.

Nobody wanted me. Nobody wanted to get paid back for me. Nobody wanted to be associated with me. They just wanted me to go away and be forgotten as if I never was.

So my mother took me back to the shop. He bolted me on to a strong new trailer and let me rest. It was several weeks before he drilled the lock.

My floor was covered in candle wax, littered. There was a sharp smell about me. My walls were singed. There were stains in the corners. But my bones were still good.

My mother lovingly scraped and washed and dried my insides. He coated them in four layers of fresh new primer. He gave me time to forget my past, using me as the classroom of his schoolhouse, where he taught tiny housebuilding.

Later he gave me more windows, and insulated and wired and plumbed me, with a shower and a sink and a toilet. He trimmed my windows and put LED lights in my ceiling and coated me in shimmering layers of varnish, so that I sparkled anew.

I am the House of Sin. And now I'm off to live with a nice woman near the coast. I am warm and tidy and clean. I will never tell her about my past. And I will never sin again.

The Utopian

I am the Utopian. I am the first of several tiny houses on wheels that my mother built for idealists. These people did not have enough money to buy a house, and did not want to waste their money on rent. Todd and Kathy had been ministers and then teachers, raising their children and then their childrens' children. They believed in living by example. They always gave more to others than they received in return.

Todd and Kathy built their dream house on a bluff overlooking the ocean. It was small but beautiful, and they built it themselves. When they were almost done, part of the bluff collapsed in a storm. Though the house did not move, the building inspector condemned it, and the insurance company refused to pay, calling it an act of God. Rather than declaring bankruptcy they did the honest thing, and liquidated their retirement accounts to pay the bank back their $200,000 mortgage. They still had their jobs, but only $25,000 left. That's why they came to my mother, and had him build me. I am the Utopian.

I am tall and I am long and I have everything you could need. I have a shower and a kitchen and a composting toilet with a fan so that there are no bad smells. I have two lofts, one for sleeping and one for storage. I have French doors and a big deck, with planters that hold flowers and cherry tomatoes. My stairs are shelves that hold shoes and books and hanging clothes. I am a study in minimalism. Because of me, Todd and Kathy were able to save most of what they made as teachers, and within five years they had enough to buy a real house. Because of me they were able to continue to live their lives as idealists and continue to help others, even if others did not help them in return. I am the Utopian.

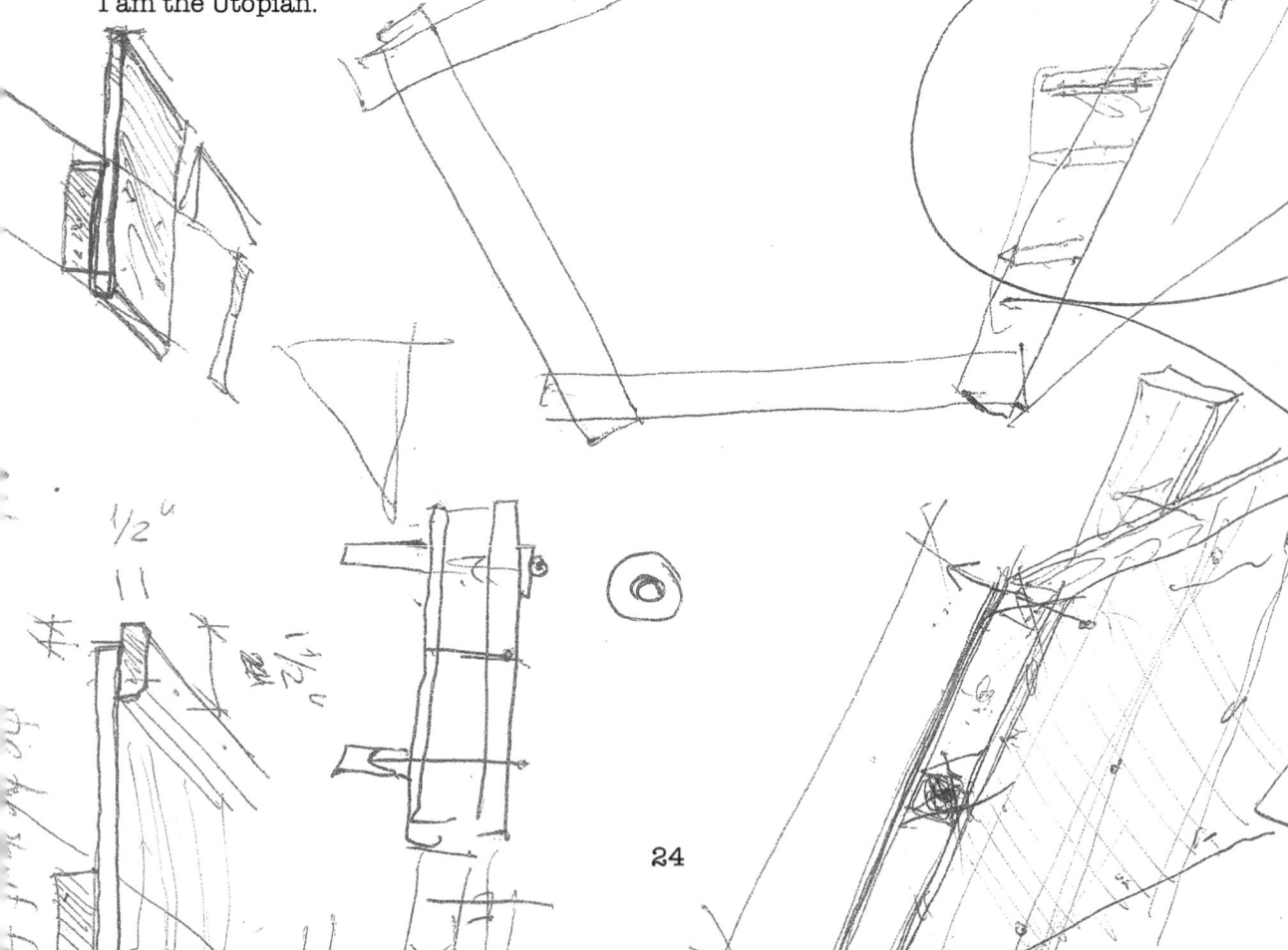

Gateway

I am the Gateway. The gateway to new hopes, new dreams, and a new future. The gateway to a place where high school and college students might build their own tiny homes.

I was the signature project of the Springfield Oregon Rotary in 2016. I was designed by my mother and the students at the Gateways High School. I was built with the help of the members of the Rotary and the students at the high school, many of whom were homeless themselves.

I was the inspiration of a hard-working teacher from a home of hard-working women. I was a collaboration between the principal of the high school, the teacher, the students, the Springfield Education Foundation, the Catholic Community Center, and the Willamalane Park and Recreation District. I house a homeless family in the Catholic Community Center parking lot. At the opening ceremony the teacher, the priest, the head of the Springfield Rotary, and the head of the Springfield Education Foundation all stood proudly on my porch. It is they who have kept me healthy and happy all these years.

I am the Gateway. I am simple and elegant, with clean lines and a sloped roof. My deck folds down on the tongue of the trailer. My windows give light and my curtains keep it cool. I have a simple kitchen and a sleeping loft. The Catholic Community Center provides food and clothing. Willamalane provides showers. I am proud of myself and of the way I came to be. I think that there should be many more like me.

Springfield Times

Hometown paper of Ken Gloor

Volume 8, Number 11 — Thursday, January 28, 2016 — 16 pages / 75 Cents

EDUCATION

TINY HOUSES
Gateways High School students build opportunities

BY DARCY WALLACE
Springfield Times Editor

Gateways High School students are moving ahead on their vision of creating one new tiny house for a homeless Springfield citizen.

All that remains, of course, is building and fundraising – no small task, as about $10,000 in funds is the minimum estimate to get the project off the ground.

However, a big step in the right direction came to fruition Jan. 22, as students chose two models as viable for a future real-life house.

Last week, Gateways students in sixth and seventh period afternoon classes designed tiny house models with the guidance of teacher Holly Ellingson and Backyard Bungalows, LLC owner Alex Daniell.

Daniell was heavily involved with Opportunity Village, the Eugene tiny house neighborhood that incorporated as a 501c3 nonprofit in October 2012 with the goal to get people off the streets and into a home to rebuild their lives and gain stability.

In recent years, tiny houses have taken off, from individuals looking to save money and conserve energy, and groups seeing the houses as an opportunity to address homelessness.

"I'm hoping this will be a way to really reach out to the hearts and minds of different parents and institutions," Daniell said. "The kids have so many creative ideas about how to design and build. And then if we can make it real for them, and actually house a person at the same time, it seems like a perfect combination."

According to Daniell, Backyard Bungalows has various models for the tiny houses, ranging from a minimalist design of about 100 square feet, to larger ones up to 200 square feet that include small utilities such as a shower fixture and refrigerator.

TINY HOUSES, PAGE 16

Photos by Darcy Wallace

At top, Alex Daniel of Backyard Bungalows, LLC helps Gateways students Vanessa Serrato and Matthew Keppers-Swan on the finishing touches of a tiny house model Jan. 21. Students in Holly Ellingson's class are hoping to eventually build a full-size "tiny" house for a homeless resident in the community.

Above, Gateways HS students Jacob Hill and Tianna Turnidge design the roof structure on a tiny house model Jan. 21. The students are in Holly Ellingson's class, which is in the running for a Samsung "Solve for Tomorrow" prize that could fund construction of a tiny house later this year. Now, GHS classes are working with local contractors to learn the basics behind building a tiny house, combining geometry and algebra and other skills.

Scrapper

I am the Scrapper. I am made of scraps. My purpose is unclear. It keeps changing. But nothing happens. I just sit here. I have been sitting here for years.

My mother has always been building tiny houses for others. So one day he decided that he wanted to build a tiny house for himself.

Of course he had no money to build me and no place to put me. All he had were scraps.

Whenever my mother builds a tiny house there are pieces of wood left over that do not get used. Sometimes a disheveled man with a decrepit trailer will pull into the shop laden with mysterious materials aged in the sun and sell them to my mother cheap. People bring in the leftovers from their backyards which they call donations. There are ancient pieces of castoff lumber in the bowels of the shop from an unknown past. And so on and so forth. Scraps.

There are disadvantages to being the Scrapper. There is no timeline for me to be finished. There is no home where I am destined to live. And my mother forgets about me often. He is very distracted.

But there are advantages to being the Scrapper. Because there is no contract and no completion date, the work takes as long as it takes. My birthing becomes less of an efficiency contest and more of what building truly should be, a practice.

My window trim is of live-edge birch from another job, carefully selected and lovingly sanded; painstakingly joined in the long rays of the after work sun. My siding is of clear cedar fence boards, hoarded over time. I am mounted on a custom trailer with California wheels someone left behind. I am friends with the chipmunks and the possum, the blackberry vines and the wasps and the bees. I am the Scrapper, and I am free.

Deluxe Lean To

I am the Deluxe Lean To. I have a long windowed dormer, an overhanging porch, a raised loft, Asian style outrigger beams for copper enshrined Hindu sculptures, and an inset desk nook beneath a stained glass window.

I was built with the blessings of Will Dixon Architects in front of their old offices in the Anarchists' Tea House, known as Izzy's, which they rented from the Orthodox Russian Church next door. I was built in their tiny front yard, right on the street where the hoodlums reign, across from the ice cream shop and the beer garden.

The first fellow to live in me was a homeless parishioner named John, who smoked cigarettes and threw the butts in front of the ice cream shop so that didn't work out. Then the church father realized that I was in the pathway of their all-night Christmas and Easter candlelight processions, so I had to be moved. It was the first of many moves for me.

My mother did not like to move me, as I was not designed to be moved. I am too tall and awkward, with an offset center of gravity, but I have curb appeal. That's what the Big Kahuna said.

My mother and the Graduate Student from the commune and the tree planter and Robin from the shop donned hard hats and yellow vests and put flashing lights on top of their cars and stopped traffic while I was jacked up on a trailer and strapped down and moved back to the shop, beside the porta-potties.

After a year I had to be moved again. I was dragged across the potholed gravel to a corner by the chain link fence where a young British fire fighter finished off my interior with curved shelves held up ingeniously by a fire hose, and lived in me for a while. But then BREXIT hit and he had to go back to England. That's what he said.

Eventually the Big Kahuna bought me from my mother because he was afraid that my mother would go under. Part of the deal was that the Big Kahuna would have one of his builders move me to the new homeless camp. But the builder kept running off for undisclosed reasons in the middle of the move, leaving his young assistant in charge, who almost tipped me over with the forklift and broke my back. It was very scary for me.

Fortunately, at the last second my mother rushed in and supervised the move. But by the time he was done he had ruined his knee again. However nobody knows this. As far as they are concerned everything went fine.

I was finally happy at the new camp, called Rosa. The other shelters were like me, small inexpensive movable solid-walled structures. But they were a little boring, pallet houses of aluminum, all the same. Still the camp had a festive feel, with a bath house and a kitchen far superior to the ones my mother made. Finally I could breathe a sigh of relief. I was home among my peers. But then I had to be moved again.

Now I stand at the entrance to the Rosa site. Apparently I was so much better looking than the others that I had to be moved into isolation, so that they would not fight over me. I am being used as the Gate House. I hope that I do not have to be moved again.

Salmon House

I am the Salmon House, the first of my mother's grand tiny houses on wheels.

I am twenty-eight feet long and eight and a half feet wide, with an overhanging porch, an alcove for a cello, a bathroom, kitchen, and a separate back bedroom. The sculptor who my mother built a studio for next door carved a gigantic salmon head, as large as the head of a horse, out of the thickened ridge beam that reaches out beyond my deck. He carved it for free.

An elegant elderly woman from San Francisco came to my mother's shop and wrote him a check for sixteen thousand dollars straight away. My mother got excited and went all out. But of course sixteen thousand dollars wasn't enough. So my mother and the tree planter who helped him made about four dollars an hour.

My beams are sanded smooth as cream. My walls are of glistening birch plywood shimmering with warm golden growth rings. My kitchen counter is made of a thick live-edge slab of Lebanese Cedar. My mother welded an extra six feet off the back of my brand new five ton trailer for the bedroom. It looked great, but I shimmied on the highway because I was not weighted evenly.

I was moved up into the big yard of a mansion overlooking the city, which was owned by Leona, the woman's friend, who was a hippie. Before moving me my mother asked Leona repeatedly whether there were any neighborhood covenants banning recreational vehicles. Leona assured my mother that there was no such thing.

I spent one lovely night under the stars in that place. The next morning an angry red faced man who lived in the mansion next door came stomping down the driveway waving papers. He was a retired dean of a business school, and he had two copies of the neighborhood covenant banning tiny houses right in his hand.

So my mother had to move me again, this time to the back yard of a retired man who lived near the highway. I live there now, my salmon head raised high to the sky, while the elegant elderly woman makes art in the living room and plays her cello in the alcove. I am happy here with the elegant woman, but I was happier up on the hill. Still, I am proud of myself. I am the Salmon House.

The Family Bus

I am a forty foot long twenty year old yellow school bus. Though I have been retired from the fleet I am still strong. I have been well maintained. My motor has only 150,000 miles on it, and is designed to run half a million. My mother has turned me into a home for a homeless family.

Leo, a friend of my mother's, convinced the Ashland Oregon School District to donate me for this purpose. Leo, a corporate consultant, guitarist, writer, and son of a movie star, moved up from Los Angeles to Ashland Oregon. He knew how to get on the news, and in the paper, and on the radio.

Before hiring me Leo and his girlfriend built their first bus for $40,000. They agreed to pay my mother $25,000 to build the next one. They found a darling homeless family with two beautiful kids and moved them into their bus. Leo's girlfriend had been in television, and toured the country interviewing homeless people. Money came flowing in.

It felt good to be remade. My front end became a kitchen with a study nook. My middle became a bathroom with two tiny bedrooms. My rear end became a spacious suite.

Talk shows were booked. Festivals were arranged. The Christian Broadcasting Network flew in a crew from Virginia Beach. They filmed my mother working and praying with ministers, giving thanks. Leo gave a beautiful speech. They still show the TV spot every Thanksgiving.

But $25,000 was not enough to build me to the standards expected, and too many promises were made. Construction volunteers were scarce, because old school buses with homeless families on the West Coast have a bad name. And then the Covid came.

Still I am proud of myself. I am The Family Bus. I am solid and well built, with dimmable lights and good heat and hot running water. I have been giving solace from the day I was delivered, from the heat and the cold, from the rain and the fires, from life on the street.

I am The Family Bus. I do not care about human beings. Human beings are so self absorbed. What my mother went through to build me, how much I cost, who takes credit, none of it matters. What matters is that I exist, and that I am providing shelter. I am proud of myself. I am The Family Bus.

35

Julie's Temple

I am Julie's Temple. I was created out of desperation. Out of angst. Without purpose. From a passionate need. That's me. Julie's Temple.

My mother was desperate. There was a junk collector renting space in the warehouse who took a dislike to my mother and kept dumping junk in his workspace by accident. My mother almost got into a fist fight with him before he was evicted.

There was an alcoholic who was renting the bay right next door, who thought that my mother's space was his. One night he took a chain saw to one of my mother's buildings.

My mother had a very talented worker, a lovely man, who worked with him for two years. But one day his friends came over and they got drunk. My mother's landlord was very concerned, after all the trouble it had taken him to evict the junk man and the alcoholic, and he wanted to know more. So my mother had to fire his friend, who did a lot of the hard work, and who my mother liked very much.

Plus my mother had to keep flying back east, because his mother was dying, while he was trying to finish a contract for six tiny houses at the Big Kahuna's new Tiny House Village, Emerald Village Eugene. So my mother went a little bit mad.

In his madness he stayed up late building a crazy structure in the back of the shop. I sat in the dust there for four years. Then one day Julie and Jim, who my mother knew from the New Zone Art Gallery where my mother showed his art, came by the shop and fell in love with me. My mother agreed to turn me into an art studio for Julie and also to build a sound studio for Jim. So miracle of miracles I, a strange cross between a chicken coop and a Japanese pavilion, was moved to a beautiful back yard in the south hills.

I was adorned with mahogany and teak, given a lavish bathroom and a custom kitchen, coated with layer upon layer of crystalline lacquer, and fitted out with the best of Julie's glimmering inspirational art. I serve as a guest house for visiting family and a place for Julie to be herself.

It is said that all civilization is a result of fiction. That humankind imagines things for mysterious reasons, and that this seeing is why all the man-made world comes to be. Sometimes seeings are compelled by desperation. When Jesus was in the garden he was desperate, knowing that his days were numbered, and he said: "What you do unto the least of my brethren you do unto me." Words that have trickled down through all of us and inspired us to build tiny houses for the homeless.

In a desperate moment, frustrated by the limitations of his life, my mother snapped, went mad, and built me. I have a lovely life. I am Julie's Temple.

Uncle Tom's Cabin

I am Uncle Tom's cabin. I am light and bright, with many windows. I am very easy to warm up inside. I have no skeleton, like my siblings. My walls are built of Structural Insulated Panels - chip board with white foam pressed in between like an ice cream sandwich. My walls are very strong. I was the idea of Uncle Tom and my mother.

Uncle Tom is a very generous man. He gives away ninety percent of his income every year. He lives in a tiny house he built himself with his lovely wife on the old estate, and does everything himself. He saws his own boards from trees that fall in the wind. He grows his own food. He brews his own beer. He buys land to protect the rivers. He saves elegant buildings from the old city and puts them to good use. His sons are the same way. They have their feet on the ground and their hands in the dirt. They work for themselves.

Uncle Tom liked to help my mother and the Big Kahuna build tiny houses for the homeless. Using my mother's idea of building the tiny houses in pieces with volunteers, and Uncle Tom's idea of making these pieces out of Structural Insulated Panels, I was born.

Six more Structural Insulated Panel houses were built at Emerald Village Eugene, and two at Hospitality Village. The idea was good, but my mother was not very good at following through. At first he got very excited, and built big steel jigs for lifting the walls with a forklift. But the money dried up and his attention span waned. He had a relapse of the next shiny object syndrome.

But I am here and I am proud of that. I am proof that Uncle Tom's ideas are sound. It was very simple to build me. My exterior walls only require a thin sheet of siding. My interior walls are simply skim coated with plaster. My floor has only a coating of epoxy. My wiring runs through tunnels pre-drilled in the walls. My plans are stamped by a structural engineer, so I am legal. I am proof of concept. I am Uncle Tom's Cabin.

The Wanderer

I am The Wanderer. I am one of the tiny houses on wheels that my mother built for older women with a dream to be free. I, like all of my kin, am a dream. I was built especially to wander.

My back end is raised up, like the shell of a snail, to make a loft for sleeping, and a place to hang bicycles and camping gear outside up underneath. I am mounted on a ten thousand pound trailer and held together with many metal fasteners. I am built for the road. But for a long time I didn't get to wander.

My mother built me for a woman who was smart and strong but lost an eye to a botched operation. The loss of her eye led to the loss of her job which led to the loss of her husband which led to the loss of her house. I was to be the one thing that no one could ever take away from her. And I was to take her places.

But just when I was done she met a man who was strong like her, and very handsome and handy, but did not like to travel. So the two of them stayed in her trailer and the man liked to hang out in me, with his friend Ed, and drink beers. They enjoyed me, with my Atlas Cedar stairs and mahogany counter top, my soft seats and marine-grade gas grill for cooking the fish they caught in the river. They were perfectly happy, and so was I. But then the woman thought that it might be nice, since the man was so handy, that he take some work.

This made me sad. I really liked the man, and his friend Ed, and the smell of the fish cooking, and the sound of them opening beers. And I knew that the man didn't like to work. So I shouldn't have been surprised when they hatched a plan to keep from working. They decided that they would renovate me!

The thing was, I was perfect in every way. I had a sleek glass shower and beautiful trim which framed perfectly placed windows. I had custom frosted glass sliding cabinetry and indirect mood lighting. But none of this mattered. One night they ripped me apart anyway.

They would talk and drink at their new "worksite," nailing up a board here and taking one down there, painting me this color and that. Somehow, they milked this "job" for the better part of a year.

Then one day the woman got sick of it and sold me to a cute young couple with a baby, who fixed me up in a jiffy, and headed out on the road. Now I am The Wanderer.

THE 'WANDERER'
A BACKYARD BUNGALOWS Design | www.backyardbungalows.net

PERSPECTIVE
Scale: N.T.S.

SHEET INDEX	
1 / 8	PERSPECTIVE / NOTES / INDEX
2 / 8	FLOOR PLAN / SCHEDULES
3 / 8	FRAMING PLANS
4 / 8	SECTIONS
5 / 8	EXPLODED FRAMING PERSPECTIVE
6 / 8	ELEVATIONS
7 / 8	INTERIOR ELEVATIONS
8 / 8	ELECTRICAL PLAN / NOTES

GENERAL NOTES

- Verify all Dimensions prior to construction
- Verify All Equipment, Fixtures, Casework, Doors & Windows, Trim, Finish, & Paint w/ Owner Prior to Construction or Installation
- All Framing Lumber is Recommended to be K.D. DF-L #2, or Better, U.N.O.
- All Dimensions are to Face of Framing, U.N.O.
- Dimensions are to Center of Doors and Windows and Openings and Beams, U.N.O.
- All new Headers to be Min. (1) 4x6 or (2) 2x6 DF-L #2, U.N.O.
- Builder is Responsible for Verifying Compatibility of all Lumber and Metal Hardware and providing Corrosion Resistance as Necessary. For 'Simpson' Wood Construction Connectors, in most cases, Stainless Steel or ZMAX Coating is Recommended. Install as per Manf. Spec's.
- Verify all Fasteners are Compatible w/ all Connectors. (i.e. When using Stainless Steel connectors, use Stainless Steel fasteners; when using ZMAX/HDG galvanized connectors, use fasteners that meet or exceed ASTM A153.

TREE HOUSE

I am the Tree House. Unlike my mother's other children, I do not hold myself up. My walls are trees.

At the base of the mountains, beside a deep running clear water creek, is a circle of six strong fast growing cedars.

My first floor is but a deck sitting on gigantic old stumps. But my second floor is a triangle of foot wide beams fifteen feet in the air, attached with many long wood screws to these vibrant young trees. Doubled and tripled twenty four foot long two by twelves bind us together with a web-work of joists in between. Because we are circled so tightly we are one, and in the windstorms we move only slightly, and in unison.

My third floor, eight feet above the second, will be another triangle, stiffening everything further, and carrying the roof. Between the second and third floors my walls will be elegant cross members between the trees, framed out into bright stained glass windows and French doors which open on to the deck overlooking the creek.

It feels good to be part tree and part me. I feel my limbs crackle and creak, though I am very secure. I soak up water in the winter and dry out in the spring. Birds and chipmunks, bats and flying squirrels love me. I catch falling food, and am a safe place from the predators of the earth. I am the Tree House.

EVE Prototype

I am the prototype for Emerald Village Eugene.

Opportunity Village Eugene was a success, so we decided to build another village. But we needed a mascot. Something better than the tiny bungalows. So the Big Kahuna sent my mother some money and I was allowed to grow. All the people who sat for hours talking about Emerald Village Eugene think that they created me. But they are wrong. I created myself.

It was a dark time but it was a bright time. It was a cold time but there was a feeling of great warmth. It was just my mother and me, in the raining depths of the winter, under the leaky roof of our open air shop, together.

One day the Big Kahuna called my mother and said that a reporter was coming by. He called the Graduate Student from the commune too, who had the original idea for Opportunity Village Eugene, and he came down. We all got our pictures in the paper.

I am tall and slender, with a high peaked roof and long curved rafters. My front facade juts in and my overhang juts out, giving me curb appeal. My inside walls are clad in the most luxurious of hand picked cabinet grade maple plywood, its swooping growth rings gleaming, more beautiful than any man-made creation.

I am tightly insulated, lovingly stained, and stitched together with a great many screws, so that my back would not break when I was picked up with a forklift and moved. I was not easy to move.

But I am safe now, front and center, the best of all the tiny houses at Opportunity Village Eugene, though an ugly duckling compared to the masterpieces built by a dozen different architects at EVE. I would much rather be a big fish in a small pond. I am the EVE Prototype.

Dragon Houses

We are the Dragon Houses. We are the first and last. We breathe fire.

When my mother landed in this wacky west coast town, a town of dreamers who make things real, he was not a young man. But he was not an old man either. He had been different people in different places, doing different things. But now he was new. He was much as we were. Yet to be.

My mother had no work. And so he fell back once again upon that craft that had always paid his way between other careers in art and finance: carpentry.

My mother was building a deck, when a handsome young man drove up in a beat-up pickup truck. "I'll work for you for ten dollars an hour," he said. This man was a magnificent laborer, very ambitious, and worked with my mother to create the tent-like "Conestoga Huts" for the homeless, before my mother went on to build tiny houses. This man lived with his wife and son in a warehouse owned by a philanthropic couple from Los Angeles. They liked my mother, and commissioned him to build me, the first of my mother's west coast tiny houses.

I am the Dragon House, broad and strong, with a grand five-foot overhang. I live by the lake, and house WOOFERS, Willing Workers on Organic Farms, who help the California couple with their farm.

I am the Dragon House and I have a little sister. She is the same size and shape as me, but much younger, birthed two dozen houses later. She was designed and built by Uncle Tom and my mother, with walls of Structural Insulated Panels and a roof of curved rafters. She was the first house at Emerald Village Eugene, moved in one piece on my mother's gigantic trailer. She was the first and I was the first, and I was her inspiration. We are the Dragon Houses.

Art Studio

I was an old shed, with mice and wasps, rats and bees' nests, crumbling. I belonged to an old house, a shack, built with the timbers of old rotting barns, who's cellar holes are nestled deep in the woods, among the long lines of mossy stone walls that surround them. My mother found me, and rebuilt me, and I became a place for making art.

I live in old New England, in a town with the same population it had two hundred years ago. I live beside a brook, the ghosts of barns and mills and houses and farms all around me. My mother learned to build on his own by rebuilding the old house, and me. He lived here for twelve years, with his ex wife, in his old life.

Five years after moving out west he came back to me, and I thought he might stay. His new friend made an art studio of me. But when he was lured again out west he sold me, to a young family that lived the life he had lived. And now I am again a shed.

I may be a shed, but I have solid floors, and massive carrying timbers, and strong rafters, and high windows, and a wood stove, and long counters for making art. My back deck sets out over the bubbling brook. If it were not for the trees which have grown up, I could see Mount Ascutney, which inspired the great artists Maxfield Parish and Augustus St Gaudens, who had their studios in this town a century ago.

I live in old New England, and I am patient. I will watch the people come, and I will watch the people go, but there is one thing that I know. I am not a shed. I am an art studio.

The Resurrections

We are The Resurrections. There are four of us, and we are brothers. Four men live in us, under the oak trees, at the Episcopal Church of the Resurrection. We cluster around the covered pagoda, where our men meet and eat. We sing in a chorus. There is a porta potty and a shower and a sink. Our men are warm and clean and dry. One of our men just died. But he did not die alone.

We are the resurrection of compassion, of empathy, of the Magna Carta, of the rights of man. Thousands of churches across the nation teach Matthew 25: "What you do unto the least of my brethren you do unto me." Thousands of churches could have what we have: four men off the street. It is his words that made the ideal real.

We are real. More real than the building code for dwelling units, which say that we are not allowed to be. More real than the mythology that says that there is a place for everyone in society. We are an example of the truth made real.

Our mother arranged us that we could sit together, the taller brothers in back, the shorter brothers in front, that we would not block the light. We live on wheels that we don't need, so that we may be quickly taken away, should the naysayers gain sway.

The churches are dying, because people do not see their relevance. But our church is not dying, because we are relevant. We are The Resurrections.

Tiny houses, big hopes

Eugene church deepens its commitment to helping homeless

Heather's Studio

There are irregularities. A dissonant chord. A tilting window. A crooked wall. A face that is a little bit out of place.

As my mother built me, I heard him talk of these irregularities. That in the most perfect Hindu temple parts were left unfinished, out of humility and to honor the gods. That our attempt as humans, with our box like cities, to create relentless regularity, lies in the face of nature, of love, and of life. Although all my mother's children were individual and unique, still all their irregularities, in design and framing, were washed out in the finish. But not with me. For I am an intentional irregularity.

My walls are not plumb. They flare outward. My roof is not evenly peaked. My windows slope inward, and are not evenly placed. The shelves that line my walls are not of the same width. There is darkness at one end and a wall of glass at the other. I am on a sloping hill, in an incongruous spot. I am Heather's Art Studio.

Heather is an artist, and her husband is an architect. Her paintings are of beautiful women in warm colorful places, gentle and precise. She teaches her students the art of fooling the eye with light and shadow, color and shade. With irregularity she creates regularity.

I feel her, and her students, within me. They murmur and laugh, scratch with charcoal and wash with watercolors. I hold them and free them, with the regularity and irregularity. I am Heather's Studio.

Jen's Glen

In Ohio there is a glen, and it belongs to Jen. "Come to Ohio and build me a tiny house!" Jen said to my mother. My mother is old friends with Jen.

They met almost twenty years ago, when they left their old lives behind. They have dreamed of and built many tiny houses since then. I know all this because I listened to them. I am the tiny house at Jen's glen.

There was the first, the hippie shack, with a stone wood-fired hot tub in the woods of New Hampshire. There was the Diamond Peak, with triangular windows, clinging to a hillside in Vermont. There was The Garradage, in Jen's parents' back yard in Ohio. There was the Tree House, in the forests of Oregon. But there was never enough money. Then Jen got a new boyfriend.

Jen's boyfriend is a lovely handsome man, who sits in a room with three big computer screens, typing feverishly, making bank. He loves Jen. He does not love slaving before the computers. He wants to live in the woods. I know all this because as my timbers rose, as I outstretched my carrying beams which for twenty years were meant to be, I listened to my mother and Jen.

I am the tiny house at Jen's Glen. My rafters rise high above a glistening transom window, revealing the woodland light. I have a cozy kitchen and a bright sunroom and a secret loft. There is a murmuring creek at my feet, and a gracious deck with a stone hot tub.

I always knew that I would come to be. I am Jen's Glen.

Little Brother

I am the Little Brother. I am a cozy bedroom and a bright sunroom. My mother did not build my bedroom. It was an unfinished "Spot Shelter" built by students at the Gateways High School and designed by a man who used to work for my mother. This man had to get his unfinished project out of the school parking lot, so he sold it to my mother and brought it over to the shop.

My mother's business partner, who is a funny golden eyed Irish Jewess, raised the money to buy the spot shelter through a clever Go Fund Me which included a link to many odd and interesting videos on Instagram. The church that adopted me paid the rest.

My mother wants to buy more of these "Spot Shelters" from high schools that create them as part of their carpentry programs, and then build them out into beautiful eight by sixteen foot tiny houses for the homeless, just like me. Each one will be a collaborative creative project with the church adopting the house, and each will be unique. The man who used to work for my mother and now works for the Big Kahuna has a special truck with a tilting bed and an automatic winch which can pull me up and move me, so I do not have to have wheels.

I sat between two older houses at my mother's shop. I am their Little Brother. But I am growing up. And one day I will be bigger than them. One day I will stand on my own. I will no longer be the Little Brother.

The Yurt

I am The Yurt. My bones are narrow and strong and I am perfectly round, pressing outward, with a big bubble of an eye looking up at the sky. My skin is taught and thin, my frame tightened with a metal cable that snakes through my ribs like sinew. Pie-shaped slices of thick rigid insulation stiffen me, painted white. I sit on a platform of car decking, on beams cross-braced with a pattern of pressure-treated timbers bolted to sixteen gigantic concrete piers sunk into the ground. I can withstand sixty pounds per square inch of active snow load and a six point three seismic event. I have been listening to my mother talk about me.

There are many who have lived for a time within me. They were adventurers who got stuck, people in transition, those sidelined for a time by unforeseen events, guests. My inside is decorated with the colorful remnants of these people and their lifestyles; their wall hangings, the way they arranged their silverware, their furniture. The best of this remains, creating a carefree elegance that no interior designer could replicate. I hear their voices still.

I am The Yurt. I come from an ancient ancestry. I am round, the shape of the soul, and the soul can emerge more easily within me. When friends fly into the airport my mother picks them up, gives them an old car from the shop, and ushers them inside me. They sit by my gas stove and pour tea water from my sink and tell stories of the other Yurts and tiny houses they have known. They dream of villages, of small houses and big lives.

I am The Yurt, and they understand me.

59

The Virginian

I am The Virginian, the largest of all my brethren. I have a flush toilet connected to the sewer, a spacious living room with tall southern windows, a gracious bathroom and a sumptuous pocket kitchen. I am on my own plot of land, and am the only one of my mother's children larger than two hundred square feet, which is the limit of the size of an auxiliary storage unit. But I am still built on wheels, so that if somebody does complain I can escape. My Recreational Vehicle hookup to the sewer is not permanent, and my fifty AMPs of power is plugged into a nearby jack post. Nothing about me is permanent.

Every time that my mother builds a tiny house for a client he falls for a period of time into their world. The brave woman from Virginia was a perfectionist. She had had her concerns with contractors before. And so before she would make the final quarterly payment she put my mother to the test. Every time he would complete the final punch list another inspection and another punch list would emerge. My mother had no choice but to give her whatever she wanted if he wanted to get paid.

It is always interesting how some of the most tense situations produce the best results. I am the most beautiful of all my mother's children, if I do say so myself. I am The Virginian.

Angel House

I am an angel. An angel of mercy, an angel of beauty; born to bring warmth and a generosity of spirit to the man on the street.

A woman from Los Angeles moved up to Ashland Oregon, who was friends with my mother's dear friend Leo, and lured my mother down. She promoted him heavily, beyond his deserve, to standing-room only gatherings at the library, and to teach a three day workshop building me, the Angel House.

The woman promised her paying participants that they would learn everything they would ever need to know about how to build a tiny house in three days. My mother knows that no one will ever know everything they need to know. But he knew how to select the participants that could concentrate and follow orders, and he knew how to release their forces of creativity, so that I was free to build myself from the good will in the air. And that's what I did.

I am small, but I have a tall peaked roof and lace curtains. I was bespeckled with lights, draped in fairy wings, and pulled as a float, with great fanfare, in the Christmas parade. I was to be the first of a constellation of Angel Houses to grace the parking lots of Ashland's churches, but it was not to be.

I ended up on the side of the road, the first thing you see when you get off the highway. I was darkened by soot and wrapped in vines and weeds as I sank into the mud. No one lived inside me. But I could not be moved, because one of the woman's friends owned the land I sat on.

I did not mind those years, because I had a purpose. Eventually I led to other things like The Family Bus and a house for homeless mothers. Who knows how many other Angel Houses were built because of me? I will never know. But now I am someone's back yard art studio. And I am inhabited by angels.

Hobbit House

I am the Hobbit House. I was built by kids with kids for kids, because I am a kid myself.

I am fearless, and I can be whatever I want to be, whenever I want to be it. I am small and six-sided with long boathouse beams that reach out to carry my magical Viking roof. I am at once cute and cozy, clever and darling. I am a playhouse in the bushes by day and a sentinel fort overlooking the mists of the valley by night. There are toys strewn about the dirt at my feet.

I live in the back yard of a family of nine. There is a Mommy and a Daddy, four boys from four to fourteen, two large white fluffy dogs, and a soft orange cat named Simon. Simon has a secret stairway made of driftwood hidden in my wall where he creeps up into the loft when the boys are not looking. There he menaces them from on high, swiping at their scalps and retreating into the shadows, where his eyes reflect the light.

Inside I have curved walls, round windows, and a tunnel with a trap door hidden by a Turkish carpet. I have shelves of ever changing shape: puzzle pieces that can be removed and replaced. I have a deck of savage salvaged lumber with live-edge railings harvested from the wilds.

My timbers have been hacked and handled, carved and sanded, rubbed smooth by many hands. They have been painted as a ship and a car and a plane, then whitewashed and painted again. My form changes every week, when my mother comes over to teach the kids how to build things with their hands.

I am Peter Pan and I will never grow up. I am the Hobbit House.

Lychgate

I am the Lychgate. I am of an ancient lineage. My ancestors were the gateways to the great monasteries and cathedral grounds of England and Europe in the twelfth and thirteenth centuries.

My mother built me of massive old growth timbers half a foot thick and a foot wide, taken from a bridge built seventy years ago. I guard the church.

I have a high pitched roof held by these hallowed timbers let in the shape of a cross. Deep benches flank a great flat stone beneath my roof, where people would come to lay their dead. There they would sit and mourn for due time, until the priest arrived and gathered up the body for burial in the churchyard.

I was built by my mother and the priest of this church, before he moved back east. They were close friends. This priest was a man of action, who housed the homeless, living the gospels rather than just preaching them. He taught my mother of the old ways.

I am the Lychgate, the gateway between life and death, between the world of man and the city of God. I am a shelter for the soul, a place to wait out the rain, and to smoke a cigarette. I am a place that belongs to everyone. I am the Lychgate.

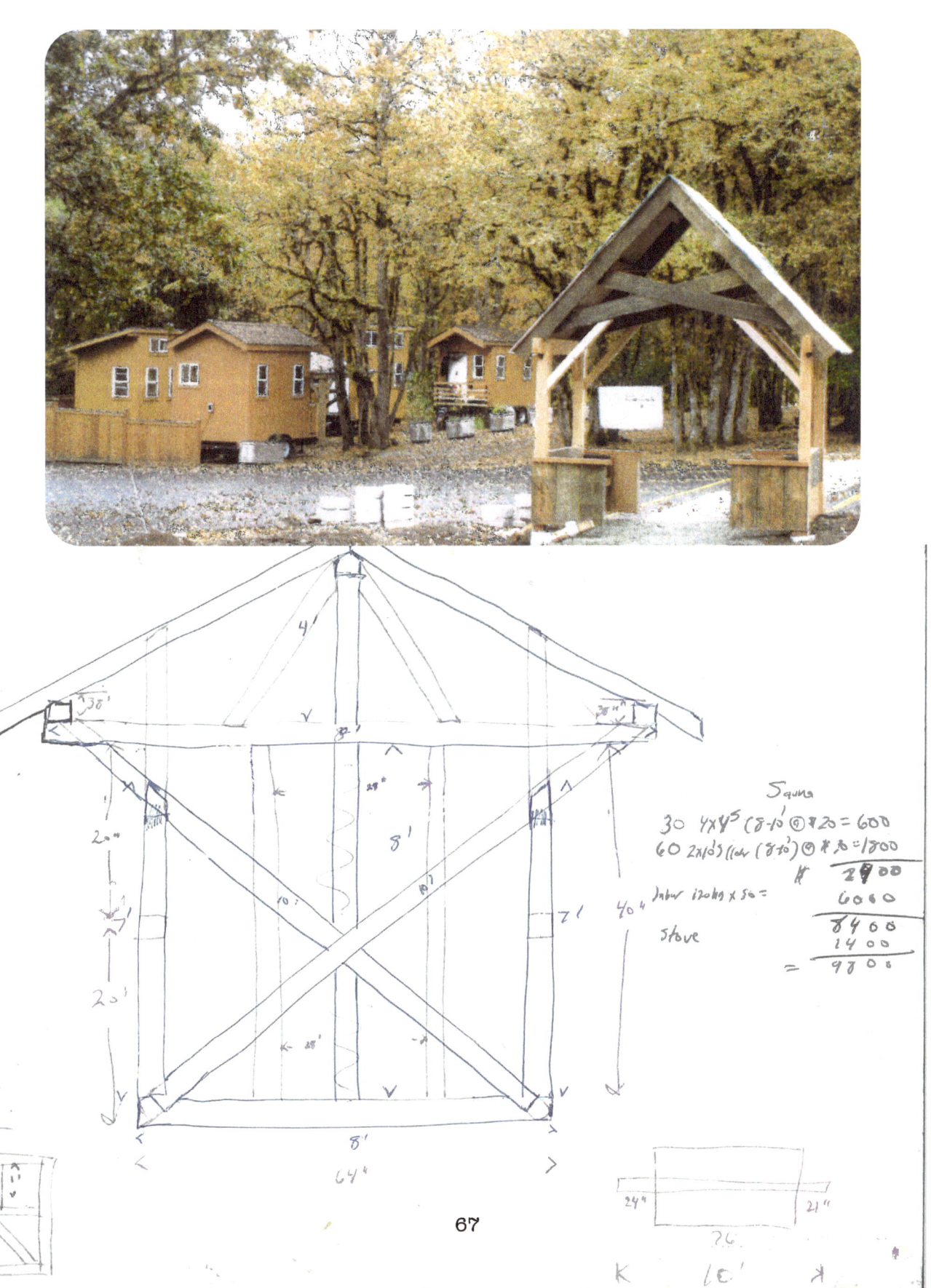

Sculptor's Studio

I am the Sculptor's Studio. Fifteen feet high and five hundred feet in size, my mother built me of the same timbers as the Lychgate, off the side of the warehouse where he rents his shop, for the wise old sculptor next door.

My great windows facing north and west warm the bright shapes of marble flowers and granite salmon, of rearing horses and Celtic crosses and bathing beauties glowing within me. Big broken chunks of Carrara marble lay scattered about outside. The studio is ever dusted in a thin layer of rock dust. There is the murmur of the running drill, the tap of the chisel, the whine of the grinder reverberating through my bones. A great fan in my forehead blows billows of white dust that rise into the air. I am a cradle of creativity.

My mother can see the sculptor from where he builds his tiny houses. They gaze upon each other through the glass. The sculptor opens his window and leans out and they talk of a number of things. They both know that the world is so full of a number of things that they should both be as happy as kings.

The sculptor is a master. A Sensei. The sculptor helped my mother make sense of his life. "Why," he asked the sculptor, "do we do this low paying work? We steal money from each new commission to pay for the last, all the while pulling splinters from our fingers and breathing rock dust."

"We practice," the sculptor told him, "so that we may practice."

I am the Sculptor's Studio. I shed the rain, close off the wind, and bring in the warmth of the sun. I practice so that I may practice.

69

Temple of Zone

I am the Temple of Zone. I was built by my mother for the New Zone Gallery, where he shows his art. I am an open walled Japanese Pavilion, eight feet on a side, held up by four posts.

When my mother's mother was dying, on the farm back in New Hampshire, my mother and his four brothers camped out on the land for ten days, to help her make her way out.

My mother stayed in his mother's art studio, with its light stained glass windows and oil paintings cloaking the walls, looking down over the pond by the oak trees, where my mother's mother was buried in a pine coffin filled with fresh grass and wildflowers, her paint brushes in her hands.

The night before she died, my mother stayed up late under the candle light, building a model of a temple in her studio. He brought it with him back to the West Coast. One day in the shop, when he was carrying the model outside the sculptor's studio, he saw the sculptor gazing at him through the dusty glass. The sculptor opened his window and they talked. They talked of what to do with the model.

"Why don't you build it full scale, and design a couple of dozen panels to fit in the roof, and have individual artists from the gallery paint each one differently? You could call it a temple to the artist."

And so my mother did. And the sculptor carved a newborn baby in the hands of the creator out of Abyssinian and lit it from within and placed it beneath me as a centerpiece.

I am a temple to the artist. I am the Temple of Zone.

Temple to the artist in us all

Alex Daniell's coming installation at New Zone is a sculpture that will display 20 additional works of art

By Matthew Denis
The Register-Guard

The scene in the back of New Zone Gallery is less gallery right now and more artist workspace. Painting a rectangular panel on the ground is Nicola V. Calvert, brown ringlets bobbing as she dips her brush in chestnut acrylic pigment. A swallow flies across the blue background while three more perch in the bottom right of the scene.

"When it's up, it'll be like they're sitting on the beam," Calvert said. "People don't often look up, so hopefully this will incline them to look above them."

The beam Nicola's referring to is the realization of Alex Daniell's vision for a communal artistic experience: the "Temple of New Zone," an eight-foot by eight-foot structure that will contain 20 paintings inside of its open-doored design.

The purpose of the nine-foot high, dual-sloping, Pagoda-roofed place of worship is to offer a cooperative space that collects art quite literally under one roof.

"I'm using this as a means where artists feel like they can belong," Daniell said. "It is very particular to Eugene, a city that is so community-oriented. And New Zone typifies this for me."

Daniell's dedication to building cooperative collectives is evident in his professional life as owner of Backyard Bungalows, an LCC that contracts with nonprofits to plan and construct tiny tracts for people needing shelter. This drive is what brought Daniell to the Emerald City.

Daniell moved back to Eugene with his partner Rachel in 2011 during the Occupy Movement, to help provide shelter for those in need. Daniell was following the lead of several influential figures in his life including Dan Bryant, minister of the First Christian Church, and Brent Wass, minister of the

See **TEMPLE**, D2

Alex Daniell stands inside his artist temple for New Zone Gallery. The structure will hold work from 20 different artists. [DANA SPARKS/THE REGISTER-GUARD]

Norman Dube, 67, begins his painting for Alex Daniell's artist temple at New Zone Gallery. The model of the temple rests on a table in front of a future piece that will make up one of the four main ceiling panels. [DANA SPARKS/THE REGISTER-GUARD]

Exhibition preview

"Temple of the Zone"
What: An eight-foot by eight-foot open-doored structure holding 20 panels that contain 20 different artists' works.
When: On display beginning Wednesday through August
Where: New Zone Gallery, 22 W. Seventh Ave.
Tickets and Info: Free; www.newzonegallery.org

MODELS

We are the children, the ghosts, the memories of things to come. We are in utero. We emerge when there is a break in the veil, at the hands of my mother, or of his students, sitting blankly at their desks with their sticks of balsa wood and miter saws and exacto knives and glue, letting us emerge.

We must be built to scale, and all the other things we would have within us built to scale too, furniture and people and pets; that mistakes and remakes be made in us, and not in the real building.

What is amazing is that if we are good-looking and well made, we may sit on the shelf for years, but eventually some client will notice us, and want us, and our shape and form will become warmth and light, cushions and cocktails, omelets and tea: a place of refuge for someone to be.

We are here, all of us, just waiting to be born. We wish that you would birth us. We are the models. And we are just waiting to be.

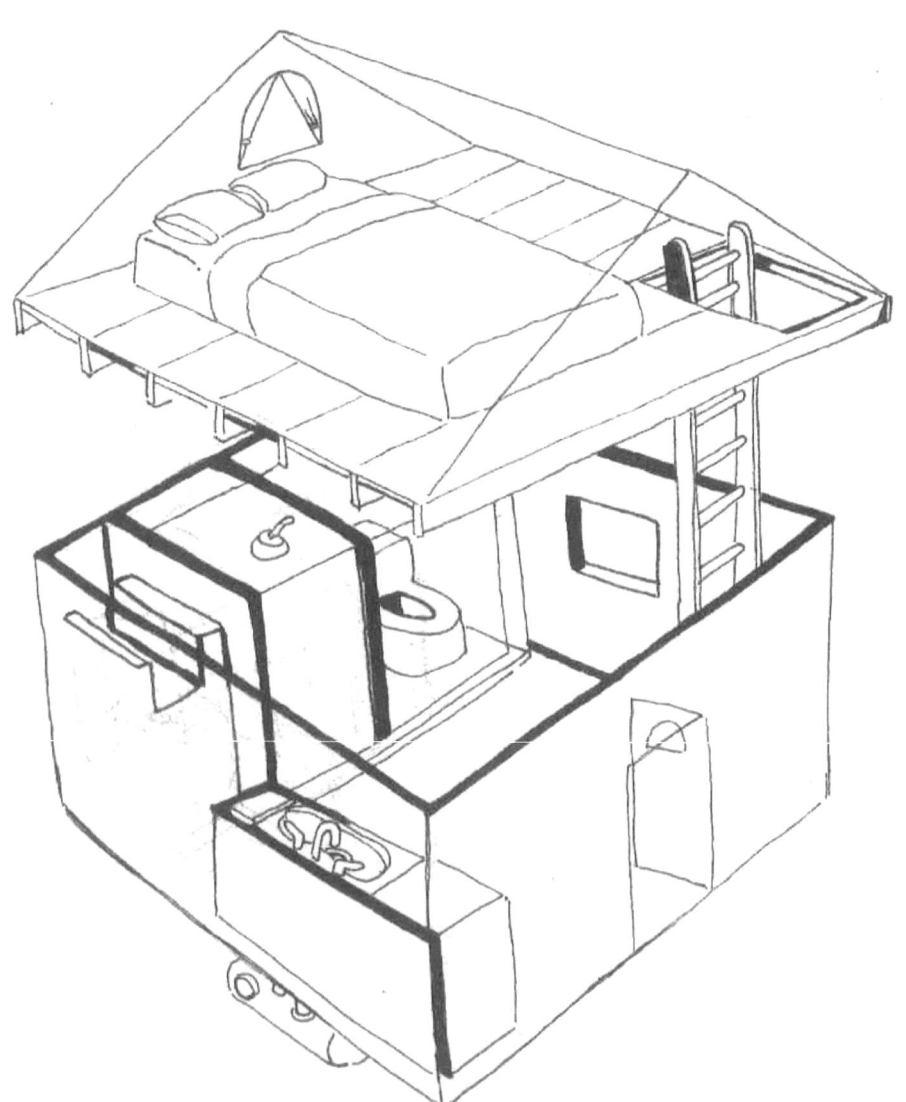

Building Villages

Panels floating. A deck of cards falling. A cadre of volunteers catching the panels and clapping them together into the form of a tiny house.

Dirt flying and pier block being set. Buckets of paint poured into trays and rolled on the walls of the buildings. Teams of students and bankers, Rotarians and church choirs, working together sorting and organizing and raising the panels of their own tiny home.

The TV reporters and the newspaper photographers, the PhD students and architecture professors, the building contractors and city officials, the ministers. The boxes and boxes of personal pizzas.

The long weeks in the shop building and stacking the panels. The first Saturday of every month another big build. The feeling of satisfaction to be actually providing shelter for the man on the street.

opportUNITYvillage
EUGENE

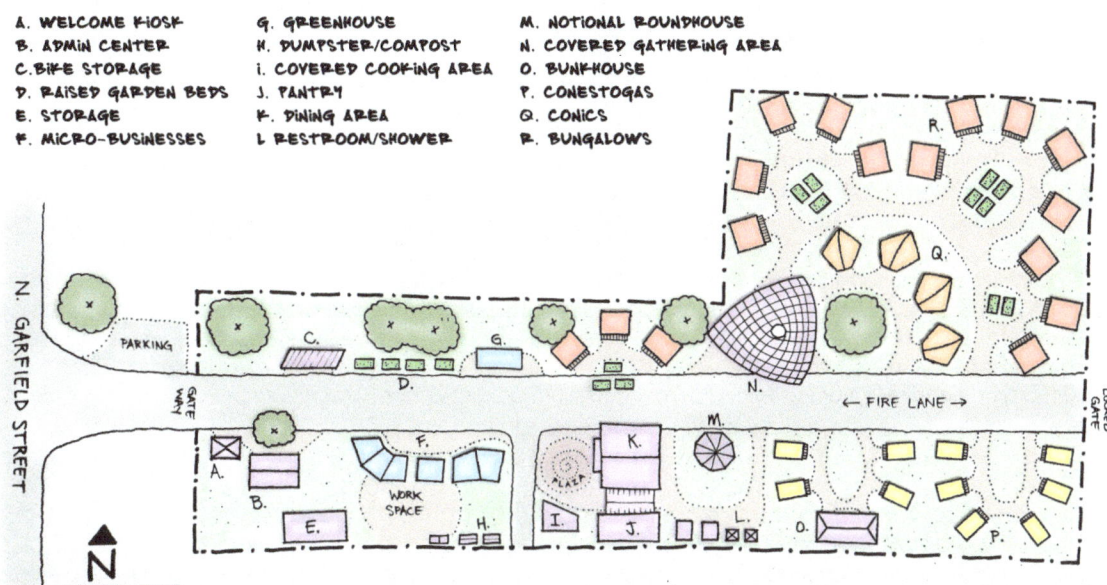

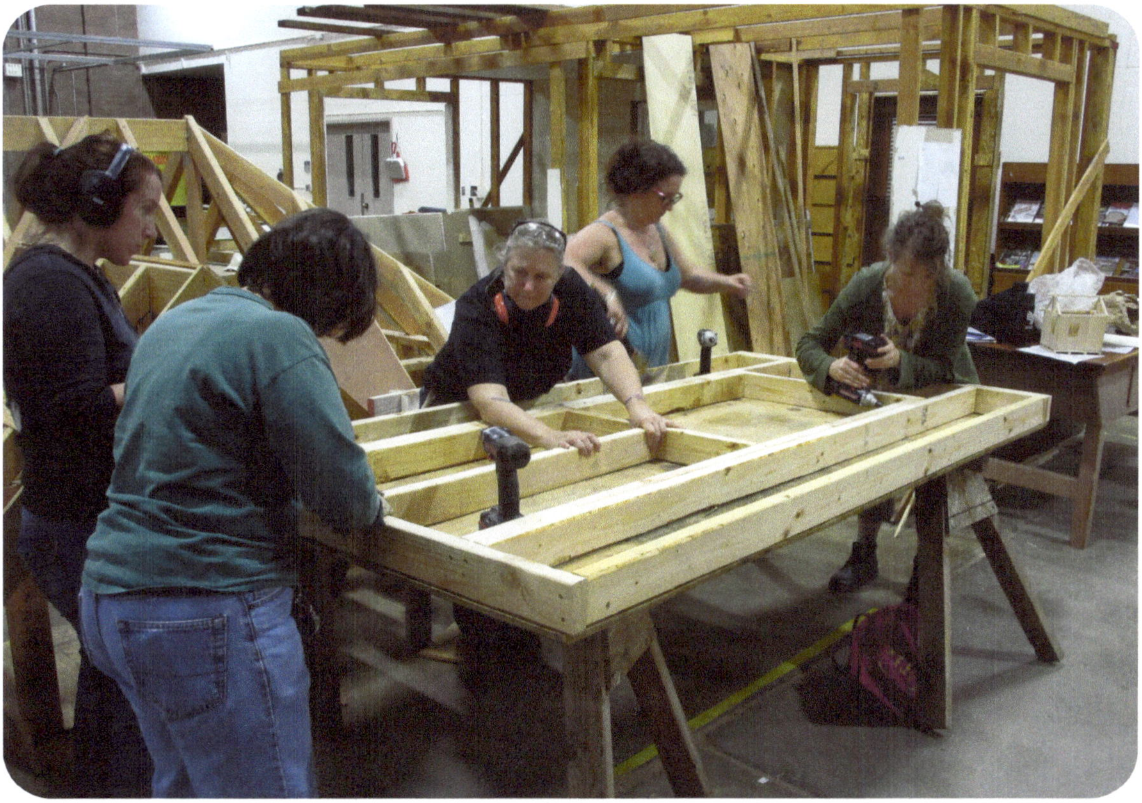

THE CODE

In this world there are codes. Codes of conduct. Rules around money. Zoning laws. And the building code.

Each year all the fire chiefs and the safety officers get together and improve the code. They require better foundations, better wiring, better sprinkler systems, better plumbing. And because of this every year the cost of shelter skyrockets. The cost of building a house has gone from $100 to $200 to $300 to $400 to $500 a square foot. And every time the price goes up it affects the number of people living on the streets.

When you build your own tiny house, always focus on health and safety. Build a strong frame immune to structural collapse. Build a solid foundation well ventilated and impervious to rodent infestation. Build fire retardant walls. Focus on a roof system with overhangs, that will keep your tiny house dry so that it lasts a long time. Focus on ventilation, to avoid mold. But think for yourself. Find innovative cost effective ways to achieve these ends. Do not blindly follow the code.

Think as Jesus did. Focus on the intent, not the letter of the law. Were the Utopian, or the Dragon Houses, or the Virginian, or Julie's Temple, or Heather's Studio built according to the code, they would have cost $100,000 to build. And if they had cost $100,000 to build they never would have been built.

Within the city limits of Eugene Oregon any structure that has a footprint under 200 square feet and an average height under ten feet is defined as an Auxiliary Storage Structure, and does not require a permit to build. Because no one can really live in a space that is less than 200 square feet.

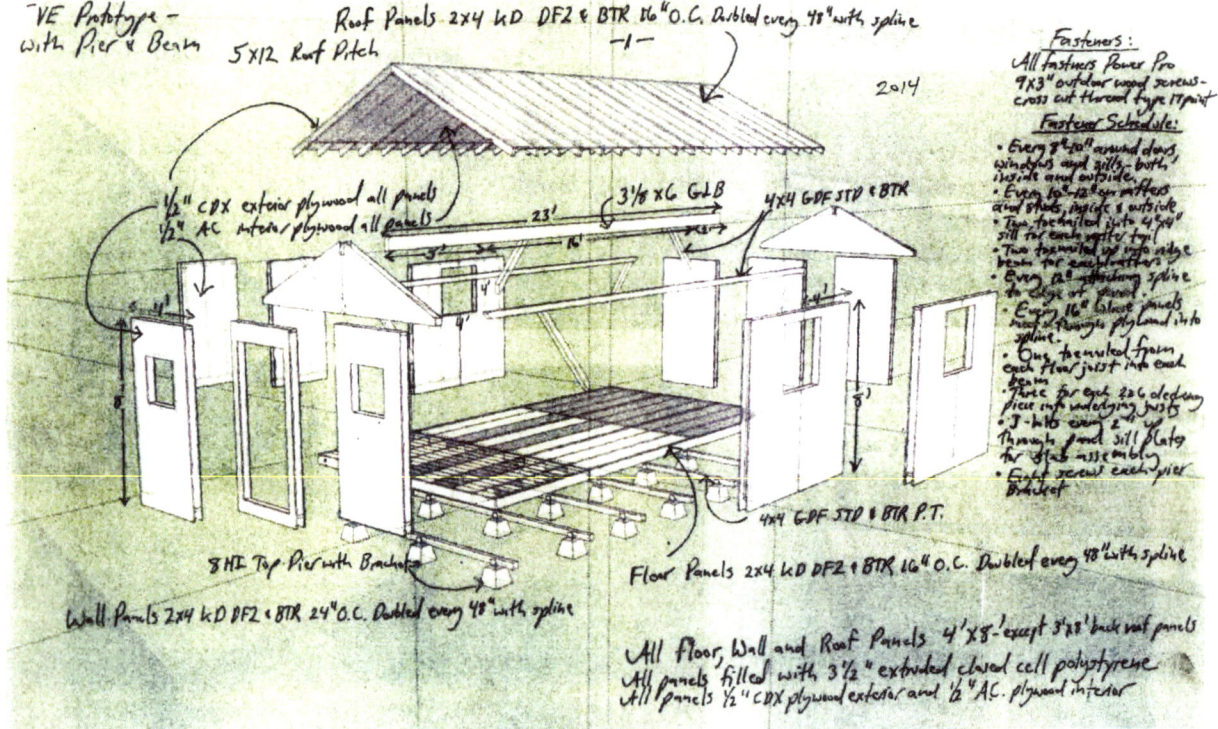

Frame your house well, and hire a licensed electrician to wire it properly. Then take it from there yourself. You should probably be able to build it for $200 a square foot, or $40,000. And if you do all of the unskilled work yourself, you should probably be able to build it for $100 a square foot, or $20,000. Be patient, careful, and do your research. Take pride in your work. Build it well.

You do not have to pay a structural engineer $400 an hour. You can exceed all the span codes in your framing and use a great many power pro wood screws to stitch it together. You can use hurricane ties on the rafters to hold the roof down and helicor anchors in the ground to hold the building down.

You do not have to wire your tiny house with two thirty AMP and five 20 AMP circuits. Four 20 AMP circuits will do.

You do not have to pay a civil engineering firm $1,000 an hour to subdivide your land.

You do not have to pay the city $10,000 in system development fees.

But you ask, why would I want to break the code? The code is there for a good reason, and I am a law abiding citizen, and I want to follow the law. I want to be safe.

You are right. Health and safety come first. A clean, warm, light, well ventilated fire safe tiny house can be yours for $100 a square foot if you build it yourself. Always remember to follow the intent, if not the letter of the law. Because there is always more than one way to do things. And if things are too expensive they will never get done at all. So just do it. Yourself.